STORM SHELTER

A REFUGE IN TURBULENT TIMES

RICHARD EXLEY

WORD & SPIRIT
PUBLISHING

Unless otherwise indicated, all Scripture quotations are taken from the Holy Bible, New International Version®, NIV®. Copyright © 1973, 1978, 1984, 2011 by Biblica, Inc.TM Used by permission of Zondervan. All rights reserved worldwide. www.zondervan.com. The "NIV" and "New International Version" are trademarks registered in the United States Patent and Trademark Office by Biblica, Inc.™

Scripture quotations marked MSG are taken from The Message. Copyright © 1993, 2002, 2018 by Eugene H. Peterson.

Scripture quotations marked NKJV are taken from the New King James Version®. Copyright © 1982 by Thomas Nelson. Used by permission. All rights reserved.

Scripture quotations marked NLT are taken from the Holy Bible, New Living Translation, copyright © 1996, 2004, 2015 by Tyndale House Foundation. Used by permission of Tyndale House Publishers, Inc., Carol Stream, Illinois 60188. All rights reserved.

Scripture quotations marked TLB are taken from The Living Bible copyright © 1971 by Tyndale House Foundation. Used by permission of Tyndale House Publishers Inc., Carol Stream, Illinois 60188. All rights reserved.

Scripture quotations marked KJV are taken from the King James Version of the Bible. Public domain.

Storm Shelter
A Refuge in Turbulent Times
Copyright © 2021 by Richard Exley
ISBN: 978-1-949106-63-3

Published by Word and Spirit Publishing
P.O. Box 701403
Tulsa, Oklahoma 74170
wordandspiritpublishing.com

Printed in the United States of America. All rights reserved under International Copyright Law. Content and/or cover may not be reproduced in whole or in part in any form without the expressed written consent of the Publisher.

CONTENTS

Chapter 1: The Cleft of the Rock........... 1
Chapter 2: Storm Warning..................... 7
Chapter 3: A Storm Shelter.................. 13
Chapter 4: Don't Blame God................19
Chapter 5: Don't Give Up..................... 25
Chapter 6: Don't Blame Yourself........ 31
Chapter 7: Who's to Blame?.................37
Chapter 8: A Scripturally Based
Action Plan........................43
Chapter 9: Lifelines:
The Word of God............... 49
Chapter 10: Lifelines: God's Character
and Faithfulness................. 55
Chapter 11: Lifelines:
The Power of Praise........... 61
Chapter 12: Lifelines: The Promise
of His Presence................... 67

I'm convinced most of us can survive any storm if we can be assured of three things. First, we must know that God cares. Second, we must be certain that God is with us in the storm, that He will not abandon us. Finally, we must be convinced that God will redeem our situation; He will bring some eternal good out of what appears to be a senseless tragedy.

CHAPTER 1

THE CLEFT OF THE ROCK

"I will hide you in the crevice of the rock and cover you with my hand."

EXODUS 33:22 NLT

A group of artists were commissioned to paint scenes depicting peace. Their paintings were then put on display in a gallery, and a show was scheduled. When the long-awaited day arrived, the gallery was filled with art connoisseurs. Slowly they made their way from painting to painting, admiring the tranquil scenes the artists had painted—a stunning sunset, a sleeping child, a meadow in the mountains, a beautiful lake, a young mother nursing her newborn baby.

One painting stood out in sharp contrast from all of the others. Instead of a tranquil scene, the artist had painted a violent storm. The sky was dark with towering thunderheads, and lightning rent the sky. The storm-driven surf crashed against the base of a rocky cliff, while gnarled trees bent before the wind. The art connoisseurs conferred among themselves, shaking their heads in confusion. "How," they asked, "can such a violent scene depict peace?"

The artist, who was standing nearby, spoke up. "Look closer."

At his insistence, they studied the painting once more. For several minutes they simply shook their heads and muttered under their breath. Finally, when they were just about to turn away in frustration, one of the ladies exclaimed, "I see it! I see it."

Pushing her way through the crowd, she made her way to the painting and pointed to a tiny bird sheltered in the cleft of the rock. Although the storm was raging, his head was thrown back, and he was singing. He was sheltered and secure in the crevice of the rock.

You may be in the midst of a violent storm right now or about to be hit by one, but you don't have to panic. Like the psalmist, you can say, "God is our refuge and strength, an ever-present help in trouble. Therefore we will not fear, though the earth give way and the mountains fall into the heart of the sea…" (Psalm 46:1–2).

Sometimes the Lord calms the storm, but even if the storm continues to rage, He calms us. He shelters us in His hand and grants us peace in the midst of the storm. "And the peace of God, which transcends all understanding, will guard your hearts and your minds in Christ Jesus" (Philippians 4:7).

PRAYER

Lord Jesus, we are in the midst of a violent storm. A pandemic is raging, and tens of thousands are dying. Businesses are shut down, and millions are out of work. Families are on the brink of economic disaster. Things have seldom looked darker, and we are tempted to despair. Protect us from the raging storm. Put us in the cleft of the rock and cover us with Your hand of protection. In Your holy name we pray. Amen.

Doubt if you must. Question if you will. But whatever you do, don't abandon the spiritual habits of a lifetime. Force yourself to go on living. Keep doing the things you know are right, no matter how artificial they may feel. Go through the motions if that is all you can do, for in time your motions will have meaning. Not all at once, but little by little, one day you discover that you'll finally feel God's presence again.

CHAPTER 2

STORM WARNING

Many are the afflictions of the righteous but the Lord delivers them out of them all.

PSALM 34:19

The year 2020 was one of the hardest years in recent memory, and I'm not sure the end is in sight. As I write this, the COVID-19 pandemic continues to rage, with a record number of new cases reported nearly every week, and the death toll is staggering. The economic and emotional fallout is taking a dreadful toll. Rather than uniting us, the 2020 presidential election created more division in the United States than any time since the Civil War. I could continue, but I think you get the point. The storm is raging, but don't despair! Let the words of Jesus encourage you. "In this world you will have trouble. **But take heart! I have overcome the world**" (John 16:33, emphasis mine).

In Matthew 7, Jesus issued a storm warning and told us how to prepare for the coming storm. He said:

> *"Therefore everyone who hears these words of mine and puts them into practice is like a wise man who built his house on the rock. The rain came down, the streams rose, and the winds blew and beat against that house; yet it did not fall, because it had its foundation on the rock. But everyone who hears these words of mine and does not put them*

into practice is like a foolish man who built his house on sand. The rain came down, the streams rose, and the winds blew and beat against that house, and it fell with a great crash."

—Matthew 7:24–27

The real difference between the life experience's of the believer and the unbeliever is not that one is spared life's inevitable storms while the other is not, but that in Christ the believer has resources to overcome the storm regardless of how severe it may be. As Romans 8:37 declares, "In all these things we are more than conquerors through Him who loved us."

To prepare for the coming storm, we must build our lives on the rock by putting the teachings of Jesus into practice. We must love the Lord our God with all of our heart, mind, and strength (Matthew 22:37). We must hide His Word in our hearts so we will not sin against Him (Psalm 119:11). We must pray without ceasing (1 Thessalonians 5:17), and we must avoid the very appearance of evil (1 Thessalonians 5:22). Finally, we must build ourselves up in the most holy faith by praying in the Holy Spirit (Jude 20).

Then, when the storm comes, as it surely will, we do not despair. We do not castigate ourselves for lack of faith, or berate ourselves for some real or imagined sin, nor do we blame God. Instead, we simply recognize that as members of this human family—a family tainted by sin and death—we are subject to the inevitable storms of life. And because we know that "in all things God works for the good of those who love Him" (Romans 8:28), we find strength in Christ, not only to endure trouble and hardship, but to overcome it.

PRAYER

*Lord Jesus, help us to build
our lives upon the rock by putting
Your words into practice.
When the future seems uncertain,
increase our faith. Give us the
courage to face whatever life brings.
May Your near presence sustain us
no matter how violent the storm.
In Your holy name we pray. Amen.*

There is no formula for overcoming trouble, no pat answer for surviving the storms of life. There are some helpful principles to be sure, important things to remember: be prepared, ask for help, persevere, and focus on God, not the storm. Still, if you put all of those principles together and shake them down, you will end up with one undergirding truth: **Have faith in God!** *As long as we have faith in God, we can face anything. We can overcome any trouble. We can survive any storm.*

CHAPTER 3

A Storm Shelter

*Whoever dwells in the shelter of the Most High will rest in the shadow of the Almighty. I will say of the L*ORD*, "He is my refuge and my fortress, my God, in whom I trust."*

PSALM 91:1–2

Having lived in "tornado alley" for a number of years, I am well acquainted with those deadly storms. There is much about them I do not understand, but there is one thing of which I am certain—if you wait until a tornado touches down, it is too late to build a storm shelter. If you hope to survive an F3 tornado, let alone an F4 or F5 tornado, you will have to prepare in advance. It's equally true that to overcome the inevitable storms life brings, you must build your storm shelter before trouble strikes.

So, what can we do?

One: Recognize storms are inevitable. No matter how well things are going right now, you can be sure a storm is brewing. That's not negative thinking. It's reality! Jesus said, "In this world you will have trouble [storms]" (John 16:33).

Two: Prepare now. We cannot prevent the storms of life—accidents, disease, death, heartache, broken relationships, and personal failures—but we can prepare for them. Daily prayer, regular Bible study, worship, and fellowship are the best ways to prepare. The disciplines of a lifetime are what will sustain you when the storms come.

Three: Be assured that God will not abandon you. When trouble comes, the storm is often so severe that it blinds us to God's presence. It may feel like we are totally alone, abandoned by both God and man, but we are not.

In Exodus 3:7–8, God told Moses, "I have indeed **seen** the misery of my people in Egypt. I have **heard** them crying out because of their slave drivers, and I am **concerned** about their suffering. So I have **come** down to rescue them…" (emphasis mine).

In other words, God sees, He hears, He cares, and He is coming to rescue us.

Four: Never lose hope. When it seems like the storm is never going to end, you may be tempted to throw in the towel. Don't! God has a long history of intervening in the darkest hour, when the storm is at its height.

That's what He did for the disciples (Mark 6:45–51). All night they battled a fierce storm, fearing for their lives. Then, during the fourth watch of the night—some time between 3:00 and 6:00 a.m.—Jesus came to their rescue, "walking on the water." He used the very thing that was threatening them—the storm-driven waves—as a means to come to their rescue, and He will do the same for you.

Remember, the Lord is greater than any storm you will ever face and He will deliver you! You can count on it. Psalm 34:17 declares, "The righteous cry out, and the LORD hears them; He delivers them from all their troubles."

PRAYER

*Lord Jesus, forgive us for living
in denial and pretending that all
is well when a storm is brewing.
Give us faith to face reality,
knowing that we are safe
in the shelter of Your arms.
In Your holy name we pray. Amen.*

Facing the deepest despair, we do not lose hope, for we know that God loves us. It matters not how dark the night, nor how great the pain, nor how tragic the sorrow; we know God loves us. In the face of the worst that the evil one can do, we affirm, "I am loved. I am loved. I am loved! And the Lover of my soul is with me." Therefore we will not fear, for the Lord is our strength and a very present help in the time of trouble (Psalm 46:1-2).

CHAPTER 4

DON'T BLAME GOD

Then Moses went back to the Lord. "Lord," he protested, "how can you mistreat your own people like this? Why did you ever send me if you were going to do this to them?"

EXODUS 5:22 TLB

Let trouble suddenly cut us off at the knees and we may be tempted to blame God. Given the pain, the inexplicable agony of life's irrational catastrophes, we may find ourselves questioning God's character; or if not His character, then His competence. "If God is a good God," we say, "how could He allow something like this to happen? How much can one family bear?"

It isn't really an explanation we seek, but assurance. We know the Bible says that God loves us (Psalm 103:8–18; Malachi 1:2; John 3:16; Romans 5:8), but there are times when our heartbreaking situation seems to make a mockery of the eternal Scriptures. In spite of God's promises, we do not sense His presence or feel His love. Like the Israelites of Malachi's day, we cry, "In what way have You [God] loved us?" (Malachi 1:2 NKJV). Or, to put it another way, "How can You say You love us, when there is such pain and misery in our lives?"

More than one desperately hurting person has looked me in the eye and said, "I've fasted. I've prayed. I've begged. I've believed. I've confessed. I've done everything anyone has ever told me to do, and look at the mess I'm in. How can you say that God loves me?"

Perhaps you know what I'm talking about. In fact, you may be struggling with similar feelings right now. For all of your praying and pleading, nothing has changed—or so it seems. As far as you can tell, the heavens are brass. To your way of thinking, the God of grace and mercy has abandoned you. He deserted you when you buried your six-year-old son, or when your nineteen-year marriage ended in divorce. Now everything inside of you rages at the Almighty. Silently you scream, "How, in light of all of this, can I believe that You love me?"

In times like these, we have a choice. We can blame God, or we can believe Him when He says, "I have loved you with an everlasting love" (Jeremiah 31:3). We can hug our hurts and make a shrine out of our sorrow, or we can offer them to God as a sacrifice of praise (Hebrews 13:15). The choice is ours.

Be assured, though, that what we choose in the time of trouble is terribly important, for it will determine our destiny. If we make a god out of our pain and anger, it will destroy us. But if we can resist the temptation to blame God, we will discover that He is very near, even when we were sure He was nowhere to be found. And in His own perfect time, He will turn our mourning into dancing (Psalm 30:11) and restore the joy of our salvation (Psalm 51:12).

PRAYER

*Lord Jesus, help us to trust Your
love even when the raging storm
seems to make a mockery
of our faith. Help us to believe
that You love us even when
we cannot feel it. Help us to
rest in Your love at all times.
In Your holy name we pray. Amen.*

There are some who believe that God sends the storms, but I cannot conceive of our loving heavenly Father doing something like that. Perhaps He allows them. **For certain, He redeems them—that is, He touches them with His Spirit, transforming them into instruments of grace that work for our eternal good.** *Of course, this does not make the troubles we suffer painless, but it does give our pain purpose. Now, instead of viewing pain as an enemy to be overcome, we see it as an ally. Instead of fighting it, we embrace it. Not masochistically, but in faith, believing that what the evil one intended for our destruction, God has redeemed and is now using for our eternal good.*

CHAPTER 5

DON'T GIVE UP

It was so bad we didn't think we were going to make it. We felt like we'd been sent to death row, that it was all over for us. As it turned out, it was the best thing that could have happened. Instead of trusting in our own strength or wits to get out of it, **we were forced to trust God totally**—*not a bad idea since He's the God who raises the dead! And He did it, rescued us from certain doom. And He'll do it again, rescuing us as many times as we need rescuing."*

2 CORINTHIANS 1:8–10 MSG,
emphasis mine

When tragedy strikes, we are not only tempted to blame God, but also to despair. Initially our faith may be strong, but as the storm continues to rage week after week, month after month, we may be tempted to give up. The apostle Paul was caught in a storm like that. Not a metaphorical storm like the one brought on by COVID-19 and the accompanying emotional and economic hardships, but a real hurricane. Acts 27:20 describes it: "When neither sun nor stars appeared for many days and the storm continued raging, we finally gave up all hope of being saved."

When you are caught in the grip of a severe storm like that, you may feel powerless. Nothing you do seems to make any difference—not your most determined efforts, nor your most fervent prayers. If you are not careful, that sense of powerlessness will give way to a numbing hopelessness. Grief will tempt you to despair, to conclude that life will never be the same again, to believe that all is lost.

Make no mistake, that's exactly how the enemy wants you to feel. He wants you to lose heart and turn your back on the Lord. He wants you to leave the church and forsake your friends. He wants you to abandon your family and forsake your faith, but if you do, you will be lost. As the apostle Paul said, "Unless [you] stay with the ship, you cannot be saved" (Acts 27:31).

No matter how severe the storm, you still have a choice. You can choose to abandon ship, to give up the faith, or you can choose to trust the Lord no matter how hopeless the situation seems. If you choose to trust Him, even though both your emotions and your circumstances suggest all hope is lost, He will see you through. This storm will finally pass.

I don't know how He is going to turn your situation around, or how He is going to bring glory out of the tragedy you are experiencing, but I am confident He will! And until His deliverance manifests itself, you have the promise of His presence—"Never will I leave you; never will I forsake you" (Hebrews 13:5)—to strengthen you. And you have the record of His miracles to encourage you. No matter how grim your situation or how hopeless it appears, be assured that "…with God all things are possible" (Mark 10:27 kjv).

When the storm was at its worst, Paul stood up and addressed the terrified sailors. He had to shout to be heard above the roar of the wind. "**…I urge you to keep up your courage**, because not one of you will be lost…for I have faith in God that it will happen just as he told me" (Acts 27:22, 25, emphasis mine).

PRAYER

Lord Jesus, we are at the end of our strength. There is absolutely nothing we can do to save ourselves. You are our only hope. Deliver us from this deadly peril. Command this storm to cease. In Your holy name we pray. Amen.

It is easy to become disoriented when trouble strikes. The cascade of events can confuse us. Tragedy can concuss our emotions until we no longer see things clearly. During that time, the counsel of a trusted spiritual friend can be invaluable. Not infrequently, they protect us from ourselves. Their counsel can keep us from doing things that we will later regret.

him. As far as the east is from the west, so far has he removed our transgressions from us" (Psalm 103:10–12 NKJV, emphasis mine).

If we will simply be still and listen, we can hear Him say, "'I have loved you with an everlasting love' (Jeremiah 31:3), and I will not let you go."

"Oh, God," we cry, "how can You love us in our sinful brokenness?"

His voice again, nearer, more persistent. "I have loved you with an everlasting love, and I will not let you go."

"You can't love us," we protest. "We're sinful. We're unworthy of Your love."

Once more He says, "I have loved you with an everlasting love, and I will not let you go."

Finally we surrender, unable to resist His love any longer. Sinful? Yes, but loved.

Storm-tossed and troubled on every side? Yes, but loved.

Hear me. No matter how dark the night, no matter how miserable your failures, no matter how much you feel like a lump of sin, He still loves you. "For as high as the heavens are above the earth, so great is His love for those who fear Him" (Psalm 103:11).

In the face of the worst that the storms of life can throw at us, we affirm, "I am loved. I am loved. I am loved! And the Lover of my soul is with me."

Therefore, we will "have no fear of bad news; [our] heart is steadfast, trusting in the Lord. [Our] heart is secure, [we] will have no fear; in the end [we] will look in triumph on [our] foes" (Psalm 112:7–8).

PRAYER

Lord Jesus, remind us that there is no condemnation for those who have put their trust in Your finished work. When the enemy accuses us and tries to fill our hearts and minds with condemnation, renew our minds by the transforming power of Your Word. In Your holy name we pray. Amen.

The problem-centered person looks at God through the wrong end of a telescope—He looks small and far away. As a result, his life is dominated by seemingly insurmountable problems, and he is driven to despair. The God-centered person, on the other hand, focuses on God's sufficiency, on His love and His presence, and like the apostle Paul, he concludes, "If God is for us, who can be against us?" (Romans 8:31).

CHAPTER 7

WHO'S TO BLAME?

Then the LORD sent a great wind on the sea, and such a violent storm arose that the ship threatened to break up...Then the sailors said to each other, "Come, let us cast lots to find out who is responsible for this calamity." They cast lots and the lot fell on Jonah.

JONAH 1:4, 7

In my experience, the storms of life have three or four primary causes. 1) We are living on a planet in rebellion, and in this world, we will have trouble (John 16:33). 2) Some storms are a product of our own poor, or even sinful, choices. Proverbs 19:3 says, "A person's own folly leads to their ruin." 3) Some storms are caused by others. When those we love make foolish choices, we often suffer the consequences through no fault of our own. 4) Other storms are the attack of the enemy. For instance, Job 2:7 says, "So Satan went out from the presence of the Lord and afflicted Job." Of course, you can see the hand of the evil one in every storm, but in this case, it is more direct.

If your storm was brought on by something you did or didn't do—poor judgment, disobedience, or even sinful choices—you need to repent. Proverbs 28:13 says, "People who conceal their sins will not prosper, but if they confess and turn from them, they will receive mercy" (NLT).

On the other hand, if the storm was caused by the actions of others, you need to forgive them. "Be kind to each other, tenderhearted, forgiving one another, just as God through Christ has forgiven you" (Ephesians 4:32 NLT).

If the storm is simply a freak of nature, something completely out of your control, batten down the hatches and ride it out. "Therefore put on the full armor of God, so that when the day of evil comes, you may be able to stand your ground, and after you have done everything to stand. Stand firm" (Ephesians 6:13–14).

On those occasions when the storm is caused by the onslaught of the enemy, you must submit yourself to the Lord and stand strong against the evil one. James 4:7 says, "Resist the devil and he will flee from you," and Romans 16:20 declares, "The God of peace will soon crush Satan under your feet."

Remember, God is greater than any storm you will ever face, so never give up!

PRAYER

Lord Jesus, reveal the cause of this storm and help us to take appropriate action. If it is caused by disobedience, forgive us. If it is the fault of others, enable us to forgive them. If it is simply a freak of nature, strengthen us with might so we can remain strong until it blows over. If it is the direct attack of the enemy, help us to stand firm even as we submit ourselves to You. In Your holy name we pray. Amen.

By looking my fears full in the face, I realized they are no match for the Almighty. By confronting my troubles, even as I reminded myself of God's goodness, I discovered that I had little or nothing to fear. God is greater than all my troubles, and He will not let me down.

CHAPTER 8

A SCRIPTURALLY BASED ACTION PLAN

"Don't panic. I'm with you. There's no need to fear for I'm your God. I'll give you strength. I'll help you. I'll hold you steady, keep a firm grip on you."

ISAIAH 41:10 MSG

It's easy to become disoriented when we find ourselves in the middle of a severe storm. That's why it is important to have a scripturally based action plan before the storm strikes. When developing a plan of action, do not rely upon human wisdom alone; instead, go to the Scriptures. Based on the Word, I would like to suggest four steps you need to include in your action plan.

Step one: Stay with the ship. Don't abandon it under any circumstances. When the apostle Paul found himself caught in a hurricane at sea, he told the captain, "Unless these men stay with the ship, you cannot be saved" (Acts 27:31). Don't abandon your family. Don't abandon your church. And don't abandon your faith. Stay with the ship. It's your only hope.

Step two: Get rid of all excess baggage. Acts 27:18 says, "We took such a violent battering from the storm that . . . they began to throw the cargo overboard."

Decide now what you need to get rid of in order to survive the storm. Is it resentment? Jealousy? Bitterness? Hurt feelings?

Unforgiveness? Doubt? Fear? Anger? That's the kind of negative baggage that will sink your ship when life's storms come, so throw it overboard! Ephesians 4:31 says, "Get rid of all bitterness, rage and anger, brawling and slander, along with every form of malice."

Step three: Anchor your soul in Jesus! Acts 27:29 says, "Fearing that we would be dashed against the rocks, they dropped four anchors from the stern and prayed for daylight." I call these anchors lifelines, and they will keep you safe even in the most dangerous storm.

Step four: Keep up your courage. Are you afraid that your storm is too big for God? Do you think your situation is more than He can handle? Or do you think He doesn't care that you are about to drown? "Keep up your courage" (Acts 27:25).

It only takes a word from Jesus to calm the storm, and it only takes a word from Him to turn your situation around. Sometimes He speaks to the storm and it subsides instantly. Other times He speaks to our hearts, and although the storm continues to rage, we are filled with a supernatural peace.

Remember, your courage does not rest in your expertise or your resilience. They are no match for the fury of the storm. Instead, your courage must be rooted in God's faithfulness. Say with the psalmist, "The Lord is my strength and my shield; my heart trusts in Him, and He helps me" (Psalm 28:7).

A Scripturally Based Action Plan

PRAYER

Lord Jesus, we put our hope in You and in You alone. You alone are the anchor for our soul. Help us get rid of all the negative stuff we've been dragging around. If we don't let it go, it is going to pull us down. In Your holy name we pray. Amen.

As long as we have faith in God, we can face anything. We can overcome any trouble. We can survive any storm. "If God is for us, who can be against us?" (Romans 8:31).

CHAPTER 9

LIFELINES: THE WORD OF GOD

For in the time of trouble He shall hide me in His pavilion; in the secret place of His tabernacle He shall hide me; He shall set me high upon a rock.

PSALM 27:5 NKJV

When it feels like your world is falling apart, what holds you steady? Acts 27:29 says, "Fearing that we would be dashed against the rocks, they dropped four anchors from the stern and prayed for daylight." I call those four anchors "lifelines," and they are what keep us from being dashed on the rocks of despair when the storm is raging.

May I suggest four lifelines that will hold you secure no matter how severe the storm?

1) The Word of God
2) God's character and faithfulness
3) The sacrifice of praise
4) The promise of His presence

In a crisis, nothing is more important than the Word of God. Our emotions will lie to us. They will tell us the situation is hopeless. The only defense we have against our deceiving emotions is the Word. Thoughts produce emotions. If we think negative, fear-filled thoughts, we will feel fearful. If we think faith-filled thoughts, we will feel confident. Repressing our negative thoughts doesn't work. Instead, we must replace every fearful thought with the Word.

So, what does God's Word say?

"You will keep in perfect peace all who trust in you, all whose thoughts are fixed on you!" (Isaiah 26:3 NLT).

"So be strong and courageous! Do not be afraid and do not panic... For the LORD your God will personally go ahead of you. He will neither fail you nor abandon you" (Deuteronomy 31:6 NLT).

"Don't be afraid, I've redeemed you. I've called your name. You're mine. When you're in over your head, I'll be there with you. When you're in rough waters, you will not go down. When you're between a rock and a hard place, it won't be a dead end—Because I am GOD, your personal God, the Holy [One] of Israel, your Savior" (Isaiah 43:1–3 MSG).

"Who then can ever keep Christ's love from us? When we have trouble or calamity, when we are hunted down or destroyed, is it because He doesn't love us anymore? And if we are hungry or penniless or in danger or threatened with death, has God deserted us? No, for the Scriptures tell us that for His sake we must be ready to face death at every moment of the day…**but despite all this, overwhelming victory is ours through Christ who loved us enough to die for us.** For I am convinced that nothing can ever separate us from His love. Death can't, and life can't. The angels won't, and all the powers of hell itself cannot keep God's love away. Our fears for today, our worries about tomorrow, or where we are—high above the sky, or in the deepest ocean—nothing will ever be able to separate us from the love of God demonstrated by our Lord Jesus Christ when He died for us" (Romans 8:35–39 TLB, emphasis mine).

That's just a small sampling of the powerful promises God has given us in His Word. Memorize His promises. Hide them in your heart against the day of trouble. Meditate on them day and night, and they will be an anchor for your soul, no matter how severe the storm.

PRAYER

Lord Jesus, do not let this storm overwhelm us. Fill our hearts and our minds with Your eternal Word. Bring it to our remembrance every time we are tempted to be afraid. In Your holy name we pray. Amen.

Is God dead?

No!

Is my sin greater than His grace?

Absolutely not!

Has He forsaken me in my hour of desperate need?

No way!

Is there anything too hard for Him?

Of course not!

Is He a very present help in the time of trouble?

You better believe it!

CHAPTER 10

LIFELINES: GOD'S CHARACTER AND FAITHFULNESS

"Who among the gods is like you, LORD? Who is like you—majestic in holiness, awesome in glory, working wonders? In your unfailing love you will lead the people you have redeemed. In your strength you will guide them to your holy dwelling."

EXODUS 15:11, 13

Trouble often tempts us to doubt the character of God. It reminds us of all the pain and disappointment we have suffered in the course of our lives. Like an underground stream, silently cutting its way through the subterranean strata, it erodes our confidence in the Lord. So slowly, so silently does it wear on us that we will likely not even be aware of it. Then one day we awake to discover that we no longer trust God. Somewhere in the long days of pain and disappointment we have lost our faith in God's goodness. We still trust Him for our salvation, but we are no longer confident that He will take care of our daily struggles.

That is often how it happens, but it doesn't have to be that way. If you know in advance what to expect, you can take steps to reinforce your faith. Even as concrete sea walls are erected to prevent the erosion of the shoreline, you can construct barriers to protect yourself from the ravages of trouble and disappointment. Fill your heart and mind with the truth of God's Word. Focus on His character and faithfulness. It is your first line of defense.

According to the eternal Scriptures, God is immutable, unchanging, the same yesterday, today, and forever (Hebrews 13:8). James says there's not even a shadow of turning or variableness in His character (James 1:17). Paul says God loves us unconditionally—He always has and always will! "But God demonstrates his own love for us in this: While we were still sinners, Christ died for us" (Romans 5:8). Speaking through the prophet Jeremiah, the Lord said, "I've never quit loving you and never will. Expect love, love, and more love!" (Jeremiah 31:3 MSG).

God is a gracious heavenly Father who knows what we need even before we ask (Matthew 6:8). It is His pleasure to give us the kingdom (Luke 12:32). He invites us to come boldly to the throne of grace and make our needs known (Hebrews 4:16). He promises to supply all of our needs through His riches in Christ Jesus (Philippians 4:19). And He is able to do abundantly more than we could ever ask or even imagine (Ephesians 3:20).

He is touched by the feelings of our infirmities (Hebrews 4:15). When we are tempted, He is faithful to make a way of escape (1 Corinthians 10:13). If we confess our sins, He is faithful and just to forgive our sins and cleanse us from all unrighteousness (1 John 1:9). And He is always and ever a very present help in the time of trouble (Psalm 46:1).

The key to our victory does not depend upon our faith but upon His faithfulness. Even if our faith fails, He remains faithful, for He cannot deny Himself (2 Timothy 2:13).

PRAYER

Lord Jesus, help us to saturate our hearts and minds with the truth about Your character and faithfulness. When trouble tempts us to doubt Your goodness, let us say, "The LORD is my light and my salvation—whom shall I fear? The LORD is the stronghold of my life—of whom shall I be afraid?" (Psalm 27:1). Make us more than conquerors by Your mighty power. In Your holy name we pray. Amen.

No matter how bad the situation, there is always something for which we can be thankful, something for which we can praise the Lord. If we focus on that, rather than on the storm, we will discover hope, even in the midst of the most desperate circumstances.

CHAPTER 11

LIFELINES: THE POWER OF PRAISE

After beating them black-and-blue, they threw them into jail, telling the jailkeeper to put them under heavy guard so there would be no chance of escape. He did just that—threw them into the maximum security cell in the jail and clamped leg irons on them. **Along about midnight, Paul and Silas were at prayer and singing a robust hymn to God.** *The other prisoners couldn't believe their ears. Then,* *without warning, a huge earthquake! The jailhouse tottered, every door flew open, all the prisoners were loose.*

ACTS 16:23–26 MSG, emphasis mine

It's not easy to worship when you are in the midst of a raging storm, but it is absolutely mandatory. It's the only thing that can renew your faith when the situation seems hopeless. The Bible calls that a "sacrifice of praise" (Hebrews 13:15).

That's what Paul and Silas were doing at midnight while incarcerated in a jail cell in Philippi. They were offering a sacrifice of praise! I can't imagine they felt like praising the Lord, given the fact they had been savagely beaten and imprisoned in chains. Surely it would have been easier to commiserate about their wounds and the injustice they had suffered, but that's not what they did. When their pain became unbearable, they started singing—they offered a sacrifice of praise unto the Lord.

Praising the Lord in the midst of a raging storm is a choice. It doesn't just happen, but when you choose to praise Him during the storm, amazing things happen. Acts 16:26 declares, "Suddenly there was such a violent earthquake that the foundations of the prison were shaken. At once all the prison doors flew open, and everyone's chains came loose."

I wish I could tell you that as soon as you start praising the Lord, the crisis will pass, but I can't. Sometimes the sacrifice of praise stills the storm, but more often than not, the storm continues to rage, but we do not lose hope. Although praising the Lord may not still the storm, it will transform you! Faith will replace fear. Hope will replace despair. Before you began praising the Lord, the fury of the storm likely made Him seem small and far away, as if you were looking at Him through the wrong end of a telescope. Not anymore. Praise turns that telescope around. It changes your focus. The more you praise Him, the more you realize how very near He is and how powerful—more powerful than any storm you will ever face.

"Therefore we do not lose heart. Though outwardly we are wasting away, yet inwardly we are being renewed day by day. For our light and momentary troubles are achieving for us an eternal glory that far outweighs them all. So we fix our eyes not on what is seen, but on what is unseen, since what is seen is temporary, but what is unseen is eternal" (2 Corinthians 4:16–18).

"Praise be to the Lord God, the God of Israel, who alone does marvelous deeds. Praise be to His glorious name forever; may the whole earth be filled with His glory. Amen and Amen" (Psalm 72:18–19).

PRAYER

*Let all that I am praise the L<small>ORD</small>;
with my whole heart, I will praise
His holy name. Let all that I am
praise the L<small>ORD</small>; may I never forget
the good things He does for me.
He forgives all my sins and heals
all my diseases. He redeems me
from death and crowns me
with love and tender mercies.
He fills my life with good things.
My youth is renewed like the eagle's!
Amen. (Psalm 103:1–5 <small>NLT</small>)*

Because we are so independent, so self-reliant, God sometimes allows us to reach the very end of our strength before He comes to our aid. Then, in the darkest hour, when it seems all hope is lost, He speaks to us out of the storm. He comes to us, "walking on the water." When He arrives, the storms often cease, but even when they continue to rage, His very presence brings us peace.

CHAPTER 12

LIFELINES: THE PROMISE OF HIS PRESENCE

*"Have I not commanded you? Be strong and courageous. Do not be afraid; do not be discouraged, for the L*ORD *your God will be with you wherever you go."*

JOSHUA 1:9

I truly believe we can overcome any adversity, endure any storm, if only we can be assured that the Lord is with us. What we cannot bear is the thought of facing the storm alone, without Him. This is what the psalmist was talking about when he wrote, "Yea, though I walk through the valley of the shadow of death, I will fear no evil, **for you are with me**; your rod and your staff, they comfort me" (Psalms 23:4 NKJV, emphasis mine).

That's the key, isn't it? God's presence: "I will fear no evil, for you are with me."

When I was just a boy of seven or eight, I awoke in the middle of the night and thought I saw an intruder rummaging through my closet. I was paralyzed with fear, and I lay there trying not to breathe. For thirty seconds, a minute, maybe more, I couldn't do anything. Finally, I managed a bloodcurdling scream. In an instant, my father came charging into my bedroom. Of course, the intruder vanished, and Dad managed to ease my fears and get me back to sleep.

Some time later I awoke again, and the intruder was back. This time he was standing directly over me. I tried to scream, but I couldn't make a sound. I lay there, more afraid than I have ever been. With a sudden lunge, I sat straight up in bed and screamed loud enough to wake the dead. Once again Dad came charging into my room, and again the intruder disappeared.

These many years later, I'm convinced that intruder was just a figment of my overactive imagination, but you couldn't have convinced me that night. In fact, after the second experience, I refused to be comforted. My father's exhortations to be brave fell on deaf ears. Finally, in desperation, he crawled into bed beside me. When he did, fear fled.

That's still the answer to life's fears, whether great or small—the Lord's presence. As long as He is with us, we can bear any hardship, overcome any obstacle, and endure any storm. Speaking through the prophet Isaiah, the Lord said, "Don't panic. **I'm with you. There's no need to fear for I'm your God.** I'll give you strength. I'll help you. I'll hold you steady, keep a firm grip on you" (Isaiah 41:10 MSG, emphasis mine).

No matter what kind of a storm you are facing, take courage, for you are not alone. Jesus has promised to be with you. "'**I will never, *never* fail you nor forsake you.**' That is why we can say without any doubt or fear, 'The Lord is my Helper, and I am not afraid of anything that mere man can do to me'" (Hebrews 13:5–6 TLB, emphasis mine).

PRAYER

Lord Jesus, these are perilous times, but we will not fear. Danger abounds, but we will not be afraid. A pandemic is raging, but we will not panic. Our courage is based on one thing and one thing alone— Your presence. As long as You are with us, we will fear no evil. Be very close and hold us near Your heart. In Your holy name we pray. Amen.

If you would like to receive Jesus Christ as your personal Savior please pray this prayer.

Father God, I believe that Jesus is Your only begotten Son. I believe He became a man and lived a sinless life. I believe He died on the cross as punishment for my sins. I believe you raised Him from the dead and that He is now seated at Your right hand making intercession for us.

I confess that I am a sinner. I have transgressed Your holy law. I have sinned against You and those I love. I cannot save myself. I cannot undo the wrong I have done. Jesus is my only hope.

Lord Jesus, forgive my sins. By faith I receive You as my Lord and my Savior. Because You were made to be sin for me, I am being made righteous. Because You bore the shame of the cross, I do not have to bear the shame of my sin. Because You died and rose again, I am saved. In Your holy name I pray. Amen

If you prayed this prayer to receive Jesus as your Savior I would love to hear from you. Please contact me at:

Richard Exley Ministries
pastorrichardexley@gmail.com

Richard Exley is a man with a rich diversity of experiences. He has been a pastor, conference and retreat speaker, as well as a radio broadcaster. In addition, he has written more than thirty books. He loves spending time with his wife, Brenda Starr, in their secluded cabin overlooking picturesque Beaver Lake. He enjoys quiet talks with old friends, kerosene lamps, good books, a warm fire when it's cold, and a good cup of coffee anytime.

You may contact the author at
pastorrichardexley@gmail.com.

BOOKS BY RICHARD EXLEY

Dancing in the Dark
Deliver Me
Encounters at the Cross
Encounters with Christ
From Grief to Gratefulness
Intimate Moments for Couples
Man of Valor
One-Minute Devotion
Perils of Power
Strength for the Storm
The Alabaster Cross (Novel)
The Letter (Novel)
The Making of a Man
The Gift of Gratitude
When You Lose Someone You Love
When Your World's Falling Apart

www.RichardExleyBooks.com